Seattle Travel Guide 2023

Discover the Hidden Gems and Must-See Attractions of Seattle: A Comprehensive Travel Guide for First Time Visitors , Culture and 7 days Itinerary.

James J. Johnson

Table of Contents

Introduction

In the Pacific Northwest region of the United States, there lies a bustling, multicultural metropolis called Seattle. Seattle has grown to be a well-liked tourism destination for visitors from all over the world thanks to its magnificent natural beauty, innovative culture, and flourishing tech economy. Seattle has plenty to offer everyone, whether you want to experience the city's lively arts and music scene, indulge in world-class food, or explore the great outdoors. In this piece, we'll examine Seattle's unique qualities in greater detail and offer some advice on how to make the most of your trip to this vibrant metropolis.

Regarding Seattle

Washington's state capital, Seattle, is the biggest city in the Pacific Northwest region of the country. The Olympic Mountains to the west and the Cascade Mountains to the east surround the city, which is located on a small peninsula of land between Puget Sound and Lake Washington.

Due to its location in the line of Pacific Ocean storms, Seattle is renowned for its cold, rainy climate. The city of Seattle is home to a vast variety of parks, trails, and outdoor recreation activities. Despite the weather, Seattle inhabitants are renowned for being active and outdoorsy.

Seattle is a significant economic engine and the location of some of the biggest tech firms in the world, such as Amazon and Microsoft. This has caused a sharp increase in population growth and urban development, which has recently altered the city.

The History of Seattle

The history of Seattle is lengthy and intricate, going back thousands of years. Native American groups including the Duwamish, Suquamish, and Snoqualmie tribes were among those who first occupied the region. These tribes made a living off the region's abundant natural resources, which included berries, salmon, and shellfish.

Pioneers from Europe and North America inhabited Seattle in the middle of the 19th century, founding a small settlement at the mouth of the Duwamish River. The mining and lumber industries were major drivers of the city's fast growth in the late 19th and early 20th centuries.

Seattle developed into a significant shipbuilding hub in the early 20th century, and during World War II, the city was essential to the war effort by producing military ships and planes. Seattle kept expanding and diversifying after the war, emerging as a significant hub for trade, technology, and culture.

Seattle is now a thriving, diversified city that is home to many different cultures and communities, each with its distinct history and traditions.

When to Travel to Seattle

Summertime, from June through August, is the ideal season to visit Seattle because the weather is usually pleasant and sunny and there are lots of outdoor activities available. However, given that it is also the busiest travel period, anticipate crowds and increased costs.

Considering that the weather is typically moderate and there are fewer tourists, spring and fall might also be excellent periods to travel. However, the weather can be erratic, with the possibility of rain and colder temperatures.

The least popular season to visit Seattle is winter because of the frequently chilly and rainy weather and the closure of many outdoor attractions. But if you want to go when there aren't as many people around and rates are reduced, this would be a nice time to go.

How to Navigate Seattle

Buses, streetcars, and light rail are all part of Seattle's extensive public transportation network. In addition, the city boasts a network of bike lanes and trails and a bike-sharing program.

As Seattle is known for its steep terrain, be prepared for some hills if you intend to explore the city on foot. This also means that from various vantage points around the city, there are some magnificent vistas to be experienced.

Customs and Culture in Seattle

Seattle is renowned for its forward-thinking and creative culture, which places a strong emphasis on community, sustainability, and creativity. A rich arts community is also present in the city, with several museums, theaters, and galleries presenting both regional and international talent.

Seattle is renowned for its coffee culture as well; the city is the home of numerous independent coffee shops and the origin of Starbucks. Even on the wettest of days, it's not unusual to see Seattle residents going about with a cup of coffee in hand.

Seattle's dedication to environmental conservation and sustainability is another significant component of *its culture. The city has many parks and green areas*, and it has taken the lead in encouraging alternative energy sources and lowering carbon emissions.

Travel Advice for the Seattle Area

Bring layers; even in the height of summer, Seattle weather is erratic, with the possibility of rain and colder temperatures. To be ready for any weather, make sure to bring layers and a waterproof jacket.

Explore the outdoors: Seattle is renowned for its breathtaking natural beauty, so be sure to take advantage of the numerous parks, trails, and outdoor leisure options available across the city. The Arboretum, Olympic Sculpture Park, and

Discovery Park are a few well-liked outdoor attractions.

Try the food: Seattle boasts a vibrant culinary scene with a wide variety of eateries, food trucks, and markets exhibiting regional and global fare. Try some of the city's renowned seafood as well as its cutting-edge farm-to-table fare.

Purchase a CityPASS: If you want to visit several of Seattle's major attractions, you might want to do so. A CityPASS provides cheap admission to well-known sites including the Space Needle, the Seattle Aquarium, and the Museum of Pop Culture.

Consider using public transportation: Seattle's system is dependable, user-friendly, and can help you save money on transportation expenses. Make sure to ride the Seattle Monorail for a special aerial view of the city.

Seattle is a thriving, dynamic city with something for everyone to enjoy. Seattle is a must-see destination if you want to experience the city's vibrant arts and cultural scene, indulge in world-class cuisine, or explore the great outdoors. Seattle is a city that is continually changing and stretching the bounds of what is possible because of its dedication to sustainability, innovation, and community. So get a cup of coffee, pack your luggage, and get ready to see all that Seattle has to offer.

Chapter 1: Seattle's Top 10 Attractions

There are several attractions available in Seattle, the largest city in the Pacific Northwest region of the United States, for both tourists and residents. Everyone can find something to enjoy in Seattle, from towering skyscrapers to gorgeous waterfronts. The top ten attractions that make Seattle a must-visit city will be covered in this article.

1. Infinite Space

The Space Needle is one of Seattle's most recognizable icons and a popular tourist destination. The 605-foot-tall Space Needle, which was constructed in *1962 for the World's Fair, provides breathtaking* panoramic views of the city. Visitors can use the elevator to ascend to the observation deck, which is 520 feet above ground, where they can take in the 360-degree view. A rotating restaurant is also a component of the Space Needle, providing customers with stunning vistas of the city as they eat.

2. Market in Pike Place

The Pike Place Market is yet another well-known landmark in Seattle. The market was first opened in 1907, making it one of the country's oldest farmers' markets still open today. The market has a huge selection of fresh fruit, seafood, and handcrafted items. Visitors can also enjoy a cup of coffee at the original Starbucks, which debuted in 1971, or watch fishmongers toss fish at the Pike Place Fish Market.

3. The Pop Culture Museum

A museum devoted to popular culture is called the Museum of Pop Culture, or MoPOP. The museum has interactive exhibits that let visitors explore several facets of popular culture in addition to exhibits on music, cinema, and television. The Jimi Hendrix display, which features items and memorabilia from the iconic musician's life and career, is one of MoPOP's most well-liked exhibitions.

4. Anchorage Aquarium

The Seattle Aquarium, which is on the water, is a well-liked destination for young families. Otters, seals, and sea lions are just a few of the marine animals that may be found in the aquarium. Additionally, tourists can discover more about the distinctive ecosystems of the Pacific Northwest, like kelp forests and tide pools.

5. *Chihuly Glass and Garden*

The Chihuly Garden and Glass, a museum devoted to Dale Chihuly's glass creations, is situated at the foot of the Space Needle. Large-scale sculptures and installations by Chihuly are among the *works* on display in the museum. The museum's garden, which showcases a range of Chihuly's glass creations against a backdrop of lush vegetation, is also open to visitors.

6. Great Wheel of Seattle

On the waterfront, there is a 175-foot-tall Ferris wheel called the Seattle Great Wheel. The wheel has enclosed gondolas with breathtaking views of the city and the mountains in the distance. The Great Wheel is a year-round attraction that attracts both tourists and residents.

7. Park, Kerry

Kerry Park is a tiny park in Seattle's Queen Anne district. Panoramas of the downtown skyline, including the Space Needle and Mount Rainier in the distance, may be seen from the park. Popular with photographers, Kerry Park is especially lovely after sunset.

8. Park Discovery

Seattle's biggest park, Discovery Park, is situated on the Puget Sound shoreline. There are forests, meadows, and beaches among the park's more than 500 acres of stunning natural scenery. Hiking the park's paths, touring the old Fort

Lawton, or having a picnic with breathtaking water views are all options for visitors.

9. Zoo in Woodland Park

A 92-acre zoo, the Woodland Park Zoo is situated in Seattle's Phinney Ridge district. Elephants, gorillas, and tigers are among the exotic species on display at the zoo. For visitors of all ages, the zoo also provides educational events and interactive exhibits.

10. Sculpture Park at Olympic

On the waterfront lies the Olympic Sculpture Park, a free public park that houses a variety of modern artworks and installations. Beautiful views of the Olympic Mountains and Puget Sound may be found in the park. The park also offers free guided tours that educate visitors about the sculptures and the artists who made them.

Seattle provides a wide range of thrilling activities and sights to explore in addition to our top ten attractions. Here are a few deserving mentions:

The Seattle Art Museum is a gallery with a collection of works from all over the world, including modern and contemporary art, African art, and more. It is situated in the heart of Seattle.

Pioneer Square is a historic neighborhood in Seattle that offers stunning architecture, galleries, and one-of-a-kind stores and eateries.

The Museum of Aviation is a museum dedicated to the history of aviation. It is situated just south of Seattle and houses a collection of vintage aircraft and relics, as well as interactive exhibits.

Gas Works Park: This park, which is a part of the Wallingford area, has a distinctive industrial setting that includes the ruins of a former gasification facility. It also offers breathtaking views of Lake Union and the Seattle cityscape.

The Fremont Troll is a well-known public sculpture that can be found in the Fremont district beneath the Aurora Bridge. The troll is a comical work of art that has come to represent Seattle's eccentric nature.

With a wide variety of attractions, mouthwatering cuisine, and a distinct personality, Seattle is a city that has something to offer everyone. Seattle offers a plethora of sights to see and things to do, from the recognizable Space Needle to the eccentric Fremont Troll. So make sure to include Seattle on your schedule if you're making travel plans to the Pacific Northwest!

Chapter 2: Food and beverage

Seattle is widely known for its gastronomic and beverage traditions. Everyone can find something they like in Seattle's food and drink culture, which includes coffee shops, microbreweries, and food trucks. The coffee culture, well-known foods, greatest breweries, best restaurants, food trucks, bars, and nightlife of Seattle will all be covered in this article.

Culture of Seattle Coffee

It comes as no surprise that Seattle is home to several renowned coffee shops given the city's reputation for its coffee culture. Starbucks is among the most well-known coffee businesses in Seattle. Since the first Starbucks store originally opened in Pike Place Market in 1971, thousands of locations have sprouted up all over the world. Tully's Coffee, which opened its first location in 1992 and has since expanded to include more than 100 locations around the country, is another well-known coffee shop in Seattle.

Seattle is home to several independently owned coffee shops in addition to these well-known coffee companies. *Espresso Vivace, Victrola Coffee Roasters, and Cafe* Vita are a few of Seattle's most well-known independent coffee businesses. These coffee shops have a reputation for delivering excellent coffee and have a welcoming amb nice ideal for unwinding on a weekend.

Popular Seattle Cuisine

Seattle is renowned for its distinctive and delectable cuisine. The Seattle-style hot dog is one of the most well-known meals from that city. Both residents and visitors enjoy the cream cheese and grilled onions that come with this hot dog. crab is yet another well-known dish from Seattle. The popular seafood dish made with this native to the Pacific Northwest crab is offered in many of Seattle's seafood establishments.

Several renowned eateries for their cuisine are also located in Seattle. Canlis, one of these eateries, has been providing great dining fare for almost 70 years. The Pink Door, another well-known eatery in Seattle, offers Italian-American fare in a lovely setting. Dick's Drive-In is a legendary Seattle institution that offers delectable burgers and fries for those seeking a more relaxed dining experience.

The Best Breweries in Seattle

If you enjoy drinking beer, Seattle is a terrific city to explore as it is home to many top-notch breweries. Since it began producing craft beer in 1996, Elysian Brewing Company has become one of Seattle's most well-known breweries. The Elysian Brewing Company is renowned for its unique and imaginative beer flavors, and its brews have won numerous honors.

Fremont Brewing Company is another well-known brewery in Seattle. This brewery is well renowned for its dedication to sustainability, and they have received numerous honors for its eco-friendly brewing methods. The Fremont Brewing Company is renowned for producing popular hoppy IPAs as well.

Pike Brewing Company, Georgetown Brewing Company, and Holy Mountain Brewing Company are a few other well-known breweries in Seattle. If you enjoy craft beer, each of these breweries has a distinctive assortment of beers that you should try.

Seattle's Best Restaurants

Numerous highly regarded eateries in Seattle provide delectable cuisine from throughout the globe. Canlis, which we previously noted, is one of Seattle's best eateries. Canlis offers gourmet dining fare and is renowned for its faultless service and breathtaking views of Lake Union.

Sushi Kashiba, which is run by renowned chef Shiro Kashiba, is another highly regarded eatery in Seattle. Any sushi fan must visit Sushi Kashiba, which provides some of Seattle's greatest sushi.

The Walrus and the Carpenter, which provides delectable seafood dishes, and Cafe Juanita, which serves Italian food, are two more highly regarded eateries in *Seattle. All of these eateries come highly recommended* to anyone searching for a top-notch dining experience in Seattle because they have each received multiple awards and accolades.

The Best Food Trucks in Seattle

Seattle is renowned for having a thriving food truck industry, with numerous trucks delivering delectable street food throughout the city. The Hawaiian-Korean fusion restaurant Marination Mobile is one of Seattle's most well-known food trucks. Along with its renowned Spam Musubi, the truck is well-known for its mouthwatering tacos and sliders.

Raney Brothers BBQ, another well-known food truck in Seattle, offers delectable smoked meats and sandwiches. Anyone searching for mouthwatering barbecue in Seattle needs to stop by Raney Brothers BBQ.

Off the Rez, which serves Native American food, and Nosh, which sells gourmet hot dogs and sausages, are two other well-known food trucks in Seattle. For those searching for a quick and delectable lunch on the go, these food trucks offer a distinctive dining experience.

The Best Bars and Nightlife in Seattle

There are many bars and clubs in Seattle that provide a wide variety of entertainment alternatives, and the city also has a thriving bar and nightlife culture. Canon, one of Seattle's top bars, is renowned for its wide range of whiskeys and inventive drinks. The establishment is well-liked by both locals and visitors and has won numerous honors for its cocktails.

The Whisky Bar, another well-liked establishment in Seattle, offers more than 1,000 distinct whiskey varieties. The pub is a terrific place to spend an evening with friends because it has live music and a friendly ambiance.

Other prominent bars in Seattle include The Unicorn, a quirky establishment that provides a distinctive drinking experience, and The Zig Zag Cafe, which serves up traditional drinks in a welcoming setting.

Several nightclubs and music venues in Seattle provide a variety of entertainment alternatives for people wishing to go out on the town. The greatest nightclubs in Seattle include Neumos, a well-liked location for live music and concerts, and Q Nightclub, which plays electronic music and hosts DJs.

A significant component of what makes Seattle such a distinctive and fascinating city is its food and drink scene. Everyone can find something they like in Seattle's food and drink culture, which includes coffee shops, microbreweries, and food trucks. Seattle is a must-visit location for any gourmet or drink enthusiast thanks to the city's well-known cuisine, acclaimed restaurants, and exciting nightlife. Seattle has lots to offer whether you enjoy seafood, artisan beer, or coffee.

Chapter 3: Cost of Hotels

Seattle, Washington, is a well-liked vacation spot for both local and foreign travelers. Finding the ideal accommodations is essential to having a great vacation, whether you are traveling for work or pleasure. From affordable hotels and hostels to opulent resorts and vacation rentals, Seattle has accommodations to suit all tastes and budgets.

Prestigious hotels in Seattle

Seattle has a selection of well-regarded hotels for visitors seeking the height of luxury. These hotels offer first-rate services, opulent amenities, and breathtaking views of the city and its surroundings. The following are a few of Seattle's top hotels:

The Four Seasons Hotel Seattle boasts breathtaking views of Elliott Bay and the Olympic Mountains and is situated in the center of downtown Seattle. An outdoor infinity pool, exercise center, and full-service spa are available at this opulent hotel. Additionally, guests can eat at the highly regarded Pacific Northwest restaurant Goldfinch Tavern inside the hotel.

The Fairmont Olympic Hotel is a notable historic building in the heart of Seattle. This 1924-built hotel has excellent furnishings and traditional architecture. The hotel has a fitness center, a full-service spa, and several dining options, including The Georgian, which serves food with French influences.

Thompson Seattle: The Thompson Seattle offers breathtaking views of the Olympic Mountains and Puget Sound from its location in the hip Belltown area. This contemporary hotel has a restaurant featuring cuisine from the Pacific Northwest, a fitness center, and a rooftop bar and lounge.

Hotels in Seattle on a budget

For those on a low budget, Seattle also has a selection of affordable hotels. These hotels provide budget-friendly lodging that is hygienic and welcoming. The following are some of Seattle's top cheap lodgings:

- **Hotel Seattle**: *Conveniently located in the center of Seattle, Hotel Seattle provides tidy, cozy rooms at a reasonable cost. Many of Seattle's famous attractions, including Pike Place Market and the Space Needle, are accessible by foot from the hotel.*

- **Kings Inn Seattle**: *This hotel provides cozy accommodations at a reasonable cost. The hotel is situated in the thriving Belltown district, which is well-known for its exciting nightlife and cutting-edge eateries.*

- **The Moore Hotel** *is a historic inn situated in the heart of Seattle. The hotel provides reasonably priced lodging that is hygienic and comfy. Many of Seattle's prominent attractions, including Pike Place Market* *and the Seattle Art Museum, are accessible by foot from the hotel.*

Seattle hotels in the mid-range

Seattle has a wide selection of mid-range hotels for individuals looking for a hotel that strikes a compromise between luxury and cost. These hotels provide cozy lodgings and a variety of services at an affordable price. The following are a few of the top mid-range hotels in Seattle:

1. **Hyatt Place Seattle/Downtown**: In the center of Seattle's downtown, the Hyatt Place Seattle/Downtown offers welcoming lodgings. The hotel has a 24-hour market, a fitness facility, and free breakfast.

2. **Hotel Theodore**: Situated in the busy downtown area, Hotel Theodore is a chic hotel. The hotel offers cozy lodgings and a variety of services, such as a rooftop lounge, fitness center, and free bicycles.

3. **The Mediterranean Inn** is a hotel with a Mediterranean theme that is situated in the Queen Anne district. The hotel has cozy lodgings and a variety of services, such as a fitness center and a rooftop terrace with breathtaking city views.

Upscale lodging in Seattle

Seattle has a selection of opulent hotels for visitors seeking the height of luxury. These accommodations provide the best amenities, top-notch service, and breathtaking views of the city and its surroundings. The following are a few of Seattle's top luxury hotels:

- *The Ritz-Carlton, Seattle*: Located in the center of Seattle's downtown, the Ritz-Carlton, Seattle offers opulent lodging. The hotel has a fitness facility, a full-service spa, and several restaurants, including The Art Restaurant, which serves Pacific Northwest fare.

- One of the best-reviewed luxury hotels in the area is the **Four Seasons Hotel Seattle**. The hotel provides beautiful panoramas of the surroundings, including the Olympic Mountains and Elliott Bay. An outdoor infinity pool, exercise center, and full-service spa are just a few of the attractions available to visitors.

- *The Fairmont Olympic Hotel* is a renowned landmark in the heart of Seattle that provides opulent lodgings and first-rate service. The hotel has a fitness facility, a full-service spa, and several dining establishments, including The Georgian, which serves food with French influences.

Seattle Hostels

Seattle has several hostels for those on a budget or seeking a more social experience. Hostels provide a more social setting with shared lodging and common areas. The following are a few of the top hostels in Seattle:

The HI Seattle at the American Hotel *is a landmark in the famed International District of Seattle. The hostel provides a variety of lodging options, including private rooms and dorm-style rooms. Additionally, visitors may take advantage of the common areas, which also include a lounge and kitchen.*

The Green Tortoise Hostel *is a popular establishment in the thriving Pike Place Market area of Seattle. The hostel provides a variety of lodging options, including private rooms and dorm-style rooms. Additionally, visitors can take advantage of common areas including a rooftop patio and a kitchen that is completely furnished.*

The Belltown district, *where City Hostel Seattle is situated, provides quick access to Seattle's finest attractions. The hostel provides a variety of lodging options, including private rooms and dorm-style rooms. Additionally, visitors may take advantage of the common areas, which also include a lounge and kitchen.*

Vacation rentals and Airbnb in Seattle

Seattle has many alternatives for Airbnb and vacation rentals for those seeking a more domestic experience. These lodgings provide a variety of conveniences, like fully furnished kitchens and segregated outdoor areas. The following are some of Seattle's top Airbnb and holiday rental choices:

From little flats to opulent penthouses, **Seattle Oasis Vacation Rentals** provides a variety of accommodations across the city. Modern conveniences like fully *furnished kitchens and free Wi-Fi are included at every* property.

Stay Alfred: Stay Alfred provides a selection of vacation rentals in Seattle's city center. Studio apartments and roomy two-bedroom homes are among the options available to guests. Modern conveniences like fully furnished kitchens and free Wi-Fi are included at every property.

Airbnb: In Seattle, Airbnb provides a variety of vacation rental homes. A variety of lodging options are available to visitors, including comfortable apartments and large homes. A variety of amenities are provided by Airbnb rentals, including private outdoor areas and kitchens that are completely functional.

For visitors with various tastes and financial constraints, Seattle provides a wide range of lodging options. Seattle features accommodations for every price, whether you're looking for a five-star hotel or a hostel. You can take advantage of your trip and all that Seattle has to offer by picking the appropriate lodging.

Chapter 4: Arrangements and Price

In the American Pacific Northwest, there lies a bustling metropolis called Seattle. It is a popular tourist destination because of its breathtaking natural environment, varied culture, and energetic city life. However, just like in any large city, it might be difficult to find the ideal lodging at the ideal cost. This article will examine some of the most affordable neighborhoods, the cost of lodging, and practical money-saving advice in Seattle. We'll also offer suggestions for the top hostels, family-friendly lodgings, and options that are accessible.

Seattle's top neighborhoods for lodging

Seattle is a large city with numerous distinct neighborhoods, each of which has its distinct personality and allure. It's crucial to keep your travel plans in mind when deciding where to stay, as well as your financial situation and chosen type of lodging. The following Seattle neighborhoods are some of the best for lodging:

☐ **Downtown** *is the place to be if you want to be in the center of the activity. Many of Seattle's most popular attractions, including Pike Place Market, the Seattle Aquarium, and the Space Needle, may be found here. Additionally, it's a fantastic area for dining and shopping.*

☐ **Capitol *Hill*** *is a terrific area for young tourists and anyone interested in exploring Seattle's LGBTQ+ scene because of its thriving nightlife and diverse culture. There are other top-notch restaurants and bars there as well.*

☐ *If you want to explore Seattle's art scene, Fremont, a unique district with a bohemian air, is a terrific spot to stay. It also has some of the top craft brewers and coffee shops in the city.*

☐ **Ballard** *is a historic neighborhood on the waterfront that is ideal for anyone who enjoys seafood. Additionally, it's a terrific location for seeing the Ballard Locks and learning about Seattle's Scandinavian background.*

☐ **Queen** *Anne: Known for its breathtaking views of the city and Puget Sound, Queen Anne is one of Seattle's most gorgeous neighborhoods. Several of Seattle's most lovely parks, including Kerry Park and the Seattle Center, are located there as well.*

The price of lodging in Seattle

Traveling to Seattle is not inexpensive, and lodging costs may add up quickly. Depending on the season, the area, and the kind of lodging, the cost of lodging in Seattle can vary significantly. Here is a breakdown of prices you should anticipate paying:

1. **Hotels**: A hotel room in Seattle typically costs roughly $200 per night, though rates can increase significantly during the summer months of June through August. In downtown Seattle's downtown, a night at a luxury hotel might easily cost more than $500.

2. **Vacation rentals**: Popular in Seattle, vacation rental websites like Airbnb and others might be more cost-effective choices for extended stays or larger parties. The average cost of a vacation rental in Seattle is about $200 per night, however, costs can still be expensive.

3. **Hostels**: Prices for a dorm room at a hostel range from $30 to $50 a night, making them a great choice for travelers on a tight budget. Private rooms in hostels can cost extra, on average costing $100 per night.

4. **Camping**: If you don't mind a little bit of roughing it, camping in Seattle can be a very inexpensive choice. Within a short drive of the city, there are various campgrounds with nightly rates between $20 and $40.

How to Save Money on Seattle Accommodations

There are various methods you might employ in Seattle if you want to cut costs on lodging:

- **Off-season travel**: *Seattle is a well-liked vacation spot in the summer when the climate is pleasant and bright. However, during the fall and winter, lodging costs may be considerably less.*

- **Plan**: *As with many popular destinations, Seattle's lodging costs tend to increase as your departure date approaches. By making reservations in advance, you can lock in lower rates.*

- **Stay away from the city center***: While it may be alluring to book a hotel in Seattle's downtown, you may find better deals in the outskirts. Additionally, you'll have a chance to visit several areas of the city.*

- **Think about alternate lodging options***: Hostels, camping, and house-sitting are just a few of the many less expensive lodging options available in Seattle outside hotels and vacation rentals.*

- **Use travel rewards programs***: If you travel frequently, you might want to join a program that offers savings or points that can be exchanged for free nights.*

The Best Hostels in Seattle

Budget-conscious tourists should consider staying in a hostel, and there are several top-notch options in Seattle. Some of Seattle's top hostels are listed below:

HI, Seattle at the American Hotel is a chic and contemporary hostel with both dorms and private rooms that are situated in the International District. The hostel offers free breakfast, daily activities, and a shared kitchen.

Dorms and private rooms are available at the conveniently located Green Tortoise Hostel in Seattle, which also *provides complimentary breakfast each morning* and daily activities including pub crawls and city tours. A rooftop balcony with breathtaking city views is also available at the hostel.

City Hostel Seattle offers both dorms and private rooms and is situated in the hip Capitol Hill district. The hostel features a pleasant sitting area with a fireplace, a common kitchen, and a complimentary breakfast.

The Seattle Hostel International offers both dorms and private rooms and is situated in the famed Pioneer Square neighborhood of Seattle.

The hostel includes a rooftop deck with city views, a common kitchen, and a complimentary breakfast.

Visiting Seattle with Children

With lots of entertaining activities for children of all ages, Seattle is a fantastic vacation spot for families. There are various possibilities for family-friendly lodging when it comes to:

Vacation rentals: There are many options available for families on Airbnb and other rental websites, including apartments and homes with multiple bedrooms and complete kitchens.

Hotels: Many hotels in Seattle have family-friendly amenities like pool areas and on-site dining. Additionally, some hotels provide unique bundles that include passes to nearby attractions.

Hostels: Some hostels do have individual rooms that can fit families, albeit not all of them are family-friendly. For families on a tight budget, hostels can be a terrific choice.

Families may have a great time and save money by camping, and there are many campgrounds close to Seattle. Playgrounds and hiking trails are features that many campgrounds provide.

Seattle Accommodations That Are Accessible

Various modifications in Seattle are made to accommodate the needs of visitors with disabilities because the city is dedicated to accessibility. Some of Seattle's top accommodations for people with disabilities are listed below:

- The Sheraton Grand Seattle is a five-star hotel located in the center of the city that has several accessible rooms with amenities like roll-in showers and grab bars.

- Several accessible rooms with amenities like roll-in showers and visual alarms are available at the boutique hotel Hotel Monaco Seattle.

- Several accessible rooms at the Silver Cloud Hotel - Seattle Stadium, which is close to the stadiums and has amenities like roll-in showers and lowered peepholes, are available.

- The Marriott Seattle Waterfront is a waterfront hotel offering several accessible rooms that come equipped with grab bars and roll-in showers.

There are many lodging alternatives available to fit your needs, whether you're visiting Seattle on a tight budget, with your family, or if you have accessibility requirements. Everyone may find accommodations in Seattle, including hostels, motels, and rental homes. You can cut costs on your stay in Seattle by making reservations in advance, staying outside of the city center, and taking into account other lodging options. There are also lots of family-friendly and accessibility-friendly alternatives available if you're traveling with children or have special needs.

Chapter 5: 7-Day Schedule

Day 1: The Waterfront and Downtown Seattle

The city's business and cultural center is located in downtown Seattle. The iconic Space Needle, Pike Place Market, the Seattle Art Museum, and the Seattle Aquarium are just a few of its top tourist destinations.

Pike Place Market, one of the longest continually running public farmers' markets in the country, is a great place to start your day. Vendors can be found here offering homemade goods, flowers, seafood, and fresh veggies. Don't forget to pay a visit to the renowned fishmongers, who perform by throwing fish at one another.

The Seattle Art Museum is only a few blocks away from Pike Place Market. Over 25,000 pieces of art, ranging from modern art installations to relics from ancient Egypt, are housed in the museum's collection.

Take a stroll down to the Seattle Waterfront after the museum for breathtaking views of Puget Sound and the *Olympic Mountains. Visit the Seattle Aquarium to observe* a variety of marine life, including otters, seals, and sea dragons, or take a ferry ride to one of the neighboring islands. You can also eat seafood at one of the local eateries.

Take a ride up the Space Needle, a well-known Seattle landmark, to round off the day. The spinning SkyCity restaurant serves up delectable meals with a view, while the observation deck provides 360-degree views of the city and its surroundings.

Day 2: Museums and Galleries in Seattle

Seattle has a flourishing arts community, and the city is home to several galleries and museums that exhibit both domestic and foreign art.

The Museum of Pop Culture, which is devoted to popular culture, including music, movies, and science fiction, is a great place to start your day. In addition to artifacts from renowned musicians like Jimi Hendrix and Nirvana, the museum also features costumes and props from science fiction movies like Star Wars and Star Trek.

Head to the Chihuly Garden and Glass, a museum and sculpture garden devoted to the creations of renowned glass artist Dale Chihuly, from the Museum of Pop Culture. Large-scale glass installations that are both stunning are among the museum's exhibitions.

The Frye Art Museum, one of Seattle's oldest art museums, should be your next stop. With a concentration on contemporary art and artists from the Pacific Northwest, the museum's collection comprises works of art from the 19th century to the present.

Visit the Museum of Flight, which is nearby Seattle and offers a change of pace. The museum houses a collection of vintage airplanes, including the first Boeing 747 ever made and a Concorde supersonic jet. The museum also offers interactive displays and simulators so that visitors may get a sense of what it's like to fly.

Day Three: Seattle Gardens

Seattle is renowned for its natural beauty, and the city is home to several parks and gardens where residents may spend time outside.

The Washington Park Arboretum, a 230-acre park on the banks of Lake Washington, is a great place to start your day. *The park has a Japanese garden, many walking* pathways, and a collection of over 10,000 species from all over the world.

After that, proceed to the Washington Park Arboretum's Seattle Japanese Garden. A koi pond, a tea house, and a waterfall are among the typical Japanese landscaping elements in the garden.

Visit the Volunteer Park Conservatory, a Victorian-style conservatory that houses a collection of exotic plants from all over the world, after you've seen the Japanese Garden. There are numerous chambers in the conservatory, each with a unique climate and plant collection.

Check out the city's northernmost park, Gas Works Park, for a change of scenery. The park has a distinctive industrial design and was constructed on the site of a former gas plant. In addition to being a well-liked location for picnics, kite flying, and sunset viewing, it has expansive vistas of downtown Seattle.

The largest park in Seattle, Discovery Park, should be visited if you have time. The park, which has miles of hiking paths and breathtaking vistas of the Olympic Mountains, is situated on the Puget Sound shoreline.

Day 4: Neighborhoods and Culture in Seattle

Every neighborhood in Seattle has its distinct personality and culture. Take a day trip to some of Seattle's hippest districts.

Capitol Hill, one of Seattle's most diverse neighborhoods, is a great place to start your day. The region is renowned for its thriving nightlife, chic shops, and varied cuisine scene. Visit the well-liked independent bookstore Elliott Bay Book Company or stroll through Cal Anderson Park.

Next, visit the International District, where Seattle's thriving Asian community is located. Visit the Wing Luke Museum of the Asian

Pacific American Experience, browse the local stores and eateries, or go for a stroll around Hing Hay Park.

Make your way to Fremont, which is renowned for its quirky, artistic attitude, after passing through the *International District. Visit the Fremont Sunday Market, where* regional sellers offer crafts, food, and antique products, or check out the Fremont Troll, a huge sculpture of a troll beneath a bridge.

End your day at Ballard, a formerly sleepy Scandinavian fishing community that has been transformed into a trendy area. Explore the area's boutiques and eateries, or go to the Ballard Locks, which let boats travel between Lake Washington and Puget Sound.

Day 5: Seattle day trips

There are various day trips you may take to enjoy the natural splendor of the Pacific Northwest, where Seattle is located.

Take a ferry from Seattle to Bainbridge Island to start your day. Bainbridge Island is only a short drive from Seattle. The island features various hiking paths, a charming downtown area, and breathtaking vistas of Puget Sound and the Olympic Mountains.

Next, go roughly two hours south of Seattle to Mount Rainier National Park. Mount Rainier, a more than 14,000-foot-tall active volcano, may be found in the park. The park offers several hiking paths in addition to winter skiing and snowboarding opportunities.

Visit Leavenworth, a Bavarian-style community about two hours east of Seattle, for a change of scenery. The town is a favorite day trip destination from Seattle and is well-known for its German food, festivals, and architecture.

Day 6: Seattle's Culinary Scene

Seattle is renowned for its culinary culture, which emphasizes locally sourced foods and cutting-edge cuisine.

At Biscuit Bitch, a neighborhood favorite serving hearty biscuits and gravy in the Southern way, you can start your day with breakfast. Visit the Starbucks Reserve *Roastery next, which is the company's flagship location* and has several tasting rooms in addition to a functioning coffee roaster.

For lunch, visit Pike Place Market, where you can discover everseveraleseveralnd food stalls selling sandwiches, fresh seafood, and other regional delicacies. For a sample of their renowned mac and cheese, don't forget to visit Beecher's Handmade Cheese.

Investigate Seattle's craft beer culture in the evening. To learn more about the brewing process and try some of the best beers in the city, stop by one of the numerous breweries, including Fremont Brewing or Stoup Brewing, or go on a brewery tour.

Last but not least, finish the day with dinner at one of Seattle's many well-regarded eateries, including Canlis, which boasts spectacular views of Lake Union and serves modernized Pacific Northwest cuisine.

Day 7: Adventures & Outdoor Activities in Seattle

Seattle is the ideal vacation spot for outdoor enthusiasts because it is surrounded by breathtaking natural beauty. Take advantage of your final day in Seattle to go hiking or camping.

Visit the Olympic Sculpture Park first thing in the morning to take in the waterfront location's numerous enormous artworks and breathtaking vistas of Puget Sound.

Go on a hike in one of Seattle's numerous parks after that. Seward Park, Carkeek Park, and Discovery Park are a few well-liked possibilities. Along with miles of hiking routes, these parks also provide chances for beachcombing, birdwatching, and other outdoor pursuits.

Consider going on a kayak or paddleboard tour of Lake Union if you're *feeling* daring. This is a fantastic way to experience the city from a unique vantage point while also getting some exercise.

Finally, visit one of Seattle's many beaches to cap off your day. Popular choices that provide beautiful views of Puget Sound and the Olympic Mountains are Golden Gardens Park and Alki Beach. Bring a picnic and soak in the sunset; if the weather allows, go swimming.

Seattle is an excellent place for a seven-day journey overall. Everyone may enjoy the region's lively culture, breathtaking natural beauty, and cutting-edge food and drink scene. Seattle offers a variety of activities, whether you want to visit the city's museums and galleries, unwind in its parks and gardens, or go on outdoor excursions.

Chapter 6: Central Seattle

The vibrant commercial and cultural center of Seattle is located downtown. Numerous enterprises, stores, eateries, and tourist attractions are located there. The region is situated on a peninsula between Lake Washington to the east and Elliot Bay to the west. The International District, the Denny Triangle, and the waterfront are all about Downtown Seattle to the west, south, and north, respectively.

The Space Needle is one of Downtown Seattle's most well-known monuments. Built-in 1962 for the World's Fair, this famous tower has come to represent Seattle. Visitors can use the elevator to get to the tower's summit for sweeping views of the city and its surroundings. The Pike Place Market, the Seattle Great Wheel, and the Seattle Aquarium are some of the other well-known sights in Downtown Seattle.

Pilot Square

Historic Pioneer Square is a neighborhood in the heart of Seattle. It has the name of a Chief Seattle statue that stands in the neighborhood's heart. The original district in Seattle, Pioneer Square, is renowned for its Romanesque Revival-style buildings. There are several shops, restaurants, bars, and art galleries in the area.

The Underground Tour is one of Pioneer Square's most well-known attractions. The abandoned storefronts and cellars of the historic Pioneer Square are explored on this trip, which descends below street level. The tour offers a look at Seattle's past and the difficulties the city had in its early years.

The Waterfront in Seattle

The Seattle Waterfront is a beautiful area in Downtown Seattle that is situated along Elliot Bay. The Seattle Great Wheel, the Seattle Aquarium, and the Olympic Sculpture Park are just a few of the area's many visitor attractions.

Also available are trips by ferry to Bainbridge Island and tours of the Seattle Aquarium.

There are several piers on the Seattle Waterfront, including Pier 57. Numerous stores, eateries, and activities are located on *this pier, including the well-known Fisherman's* Wharf. Visitors can immediately purchase fresh seafood from the merchants while also watching the fisherman bring in their haul.

Shopping in Seattle's Downtown

With a wide variety of shops, boutiques, and shopping malls, downtown Seattle is a shopper's paradise. Pike Place Market is the most well-known shopping location in Downtown Seattle. More than 200 merchants sell a variety of goods at the market, including handcrafted crafts, fresh produce, and seafood.

The University Village shopping area, Pacific Place, and Westlake area are some more well-liked places to go shopping in Downtown Seattle. Pacific Place is a more premium shopping area with high-end businesses like Tiffany & Co. and Barneys New York, while the Westlake area is a sizable mall situated in the core of Downtown Seattle.

Northwest Museum of Art

One of the biggest art museums in the Pacific Northwest is the Seattle Art Museum (SAM). The museum, which is in Downtown Seattle, houses a varied collection of artwork from several countries. American, Asian, African, and European art, as well as modern and contemporary works, are all represented in the museum's collection.

The Porcelain Room is among the most well-liked displays of the Seattle Art Museum. More than a thousand porcelain items from many countries, including China, Japan, and Europe, are on display in this exhibition. The museum's collection of Native American and African art also has some noteworthy displays.

Central Library of Seattle

One of Seattle's most famous structures is the Seattle Central Library. Rem Koolhaas, a Dutch architect, created the library, which debuted in 2004. The structure has earned multiple architectural honors and has a distinctive glass and steel style.

With over 2 million visits a year, the Seattle Central Library is among the busiest libraries in the country. Along with a sizable selection of books, DVDs, and other media, the library also offers free Wi-Fi, computer access, and study areas.

Seattle's Famous Structures and Architecture

Seattle is renowned for its distinctive and varied architecture, which includes a blend of old and new structures. In Seattle, some of the most well-known structures are:

- **The Space Needle** *is Seattle's most recognizable landmark and is known all over the world. The tower has a distinctive space-age style and was constructed for the* 1962 World's Fair.

- **Smith Tower***: Constructed in 1914, the Smith Tower was Seattle's first skyscraper. Up until 1931, the tower, which has an elaborate Beaux-Arts design, was the tallest structure west of the Mississippi River.*

- **Columbia Center***: At 76 floors tall, the Columbia Center is the tallest structure in Seattle. The structure has a sleek, contemporary appearance and gives breathtaking views of the city.*

- **Seattle Central Library***: With its futuristic architecture, Seattle Central Library is one of the city's most distinctive structures. Rem Koolhaas, a Dutch architect, is credited with creating the* *structure, which is distinguished by its angular steel and glass facade.*

- **Pike Place Market***: In addition to being a well-liked tourist destination, Pike Place Market is also a historic structure. The market was constructed in 1907 and has a distinctive iron and steel structure.*

- **The Seattle Asian Art Museum** *is housed in an antebellum Art Deco structure in Volunteer Park. The structure was constructed in 1933 and has a distinctive fusion of Asian and Art Deco design elements.*

- **The Seattle Great Wheel** *is not just a well-liked attraction, but it is also a recognizable feature of the city's skyline. The 175-foot-tall Ferris wheel has a contemporary appearance.*

Overall, tourists can enjoy a variety of sights and activities in Downtown Seattle. In this thriving and lively area of the city, there is something for everyone, from historical landmarks to contemporary architecture.

Chapter 7: Seattle's Communities

Seattle is a bustling metropolis with several distinctive neighborhoods, each with its unique personality and charm. We'll look at six of Seattle's most well-known districts in this article: Wallingford, Queen Anne, Fremont, Ballard, and Capitol Hill.

Congress Hill

Just east of downtown Seattle is the crowded district known as Capitol Hill. It has a reputation for having a fun atmosphere, a diversified culture, and a lengthy history. The area is home to a sizable LGBTQ+ community and is where the Pride Parade is held each year. Capitol Hill is a well-known place for dining and nightlife because it has a lot of pubs, restaurants, and coffee shops.

The Space Needle, which can be seen from numerous locations throughout the neighborhood, is one of Capitol Hill's most recognizable icons. Volunteer Park and the old Capitol Hill Library are two *further noteworthy locations. The Hugo House* literary center and the Northwest Film Forum are just two of the many art galleries and performing venues in the area.

Fremont

A quirky, artistic district called Fremont may be found just north of Seattle's city center. It is renowned for its free-spirited atmosphere, vibrant public art displays, and outdoor markets. The Fremont Troll, a huge concrete sculpture of a troll that resides under the Aurora Bridge, is one of Fremont's most well-known icons.

Numerous tiny businesses, such as vintage clothing boutiques, record stores, and artisan food vendors, may be found in Fremont. The Fremont Sunday Market, a weekly outdoor market with locally made goods, food, and live music, is also located in the neighborhood. Gas Works Park, which provides breathtaking views of Lake Union, and the Burke-Gilman Trail, a well-liked bike and walking route that passes through the area, are two other points of interest in Fremont.

Ballard

The Seattle neighborhood of Ballard is situated in the city's northwest. The neighborhood's architecture and cultural activities reflect its Scandinavian background, which is well-known. Breweries and many seafood eateries may be found in Ballard, which also has a flourishing music scene.

The Ballard Locks, often referred to as the Hiram M. Chittenden Locks, are one of Ballard's most well-liked attractions. Boats can travel through the locks between Lake Union and Puget Sound, and spectators can observe the boats from a viewing deck. The Nordic Heritage Museum and the Ballard Farmers Market are two further prominent Ballard features.

College District

The University of Washington is housed in the University District, also known as the "U District," which is situated just north of downtown Seattle. The area is well-recognized for its vibrant environment and huge student population. Numerous businesses, including cafes, bookstores, and music venues, are located in the U District.

The Burke Museum of Natural History and Culture, which has displays of the natural and cultural history of the Pacific Northwest, is one of the most well-liked *sights in the U District. The famous Husky Stadium* and the UW Botanic Gardens, which provide breathtaking views over the neighborhood, are also located in this region.

Wallingford

A neighborhood called Wallingford is situated immediately to the north of the University District. In addition to its ancient mansions and tree-lined avenues, it is renowned for its unique mix of stores, eateries, and pubs. Gas Works Park and the Wallingford Playfield are only two of the parks in Wallingford.

The Wallingford Center, a former school that has been transformed into a mixed-use building, is one of the most famous monuments in Wallingford. A grocery store, a fitness center, and various restaurants are among the companies present in the center. The Seattle Public Library's Wallingford Branch, renowned for its distinctive design and wide collection of books and media, is another well-liked destination in Wallingford. The Good Shepherd Center, which offers a variety of community events, is another.

HM Queen Anne

Seattle's Queen Anne district is situated just to the north of the city center. It is well-known for its historic mansions and homes as well as its breathtaking views of the city and Puget Sound. In addition to having streets named for her children and grandchildren, the area is named after Queen Anne of Great Britain.

Kerry Park, one of Queen Anne's most well-liked attractions, provides breathtaking vistas of the Seattle skyline and the Space Needle. The Parsons Garden and Queen Anne Boulevard are just two of the historic sites that can be seen in the neighborhood. A variety of eateries and stores can be found in Queen Anne, especially along Queen Anne Avenue.

Everybody can find something to enjoy in Seattle's numerous neighborhoods, which range from Queen Anne's breathtaking views to Capitol Hill's thriving nightlife. There is always something new to find in these distinctive and endearing areas, whether you have lived there for a while or are just visiting for the first time.

Chapter 8: Seattle Is Family-Friendly

The American Pacific Northwest region includes the booming city of Seattle. Seattle is a well-liked holiday spot for families seeking an exciting and informative trip because of its breathtaking natural beauty, fascinating history, and flourishing tech *sector. We'll examine several of Seattle's family*-friendly attractions in more detail in this post, including the Woodland Park Zoo, Discovery Park, Seattle Children's Museum, Seattle Center, and Pacific Science Center.

Center of Seattle

The Seattle Center, a hub of activity and entertainment for both locals and visitors, is situated in the center of Seattle. The Space Needle, the Museum of Pop Culture, and the Pacific Science Center are just a few of the attractions that can be found on this 74-acre complex. The Bumbershoot Music and Arts Festival and the Northwest Folklife Festival are just two of the many festivals and events that take place there every year.

The Space Needle is one of the Seattle Center's key attractions. Built-in 1962 for the World's Fair, this famous structure has come to represent Seattle. Riders of the Space Needle can enjoy breathtaking 360-degree views of the city, the nearby mountains, and the rivers. Glass walls that reach the ceiling at the observation deck allow you to see the sights from all directions.

The Museum of Pop Culture (MoPOP) at the Seattle Center is another well-liked destination. With displays on music, movies, television, and other popular culture mediums, this interactive museum celebrates the origins and development of popular culture. The museum offers a range of interactive attractions, like the Sound Lab where visitors can try out different musical instruments.

Center for Pacific Science

The Pacific Science Center, which is located on the campus of Seattle Center, is a must-see place for families with children of all ages. The hands-on activities and interactive displays at this science museum make it interesting and exciting to learn about science and technology.

The Tropical Butterfly House is one of the Pacific Science Center's most well-liked displays. Hundreds of live butterflies from all over the world are on display in this indoor show. The display allows visitors to stroll through it and get up close views of the butterflies as they flit about. It's a wonderful chance for kids to learn about the butterfly life cycle and the significance of conservation efforts to safeguard these precious animals.

The Dinosaur display at the Pacific Science Center is another well-liked attraction. In this exhibit, visitors may learn about the past of these prehistoric animals through interactive displays and life-size dinosaur replicas and fossils. Kids will enjoy learning about the habitats, food, and behavior of these enormous animals up close.

Children's Museum of Seattle

Families with young children should visit the Seattle Children's Museum because it is entertaining and informative. This museum, which is in the center of the Seattle Center, offers interactive displays and hands-on activities that are intended to stimulate imagination and creativity.

The Imagination Studio is one of the Seattle Children's Museum's most well-liked displays. Children can use *art projects and other interactive elements in this exhibit to discover their creative side. A* range of supplies, including paint, markers, and clay, are available throughout the exhibit so children can make their artwork.

The Global Village exhibit at the Seattle Children's Museum is another well-liked one. The interactive exhibits in this space educate children about many civilizations from around the world. Children can investigate a Mexican market, a Japanese tea house, and other cultural displays to learn about the practices and traditions of people from various cultures.

Zoo in Woodland Park

In the Seattle neighborhood of Phinney Ridge, there is a 92-acre zoological park called the Woodland Park Zoo. More than 1,000 species from all around the world live in this zoo, including lions, tigers, bears, and elephants.

The African Savanna exhibit at the Woodland Park Zoo is one of the highlights. Giraffes, zebras, and ostriches are just a few of the natural African savanna creatures on display in this exhibition. Visitors can feed the giraffes from an elevated platform while watching these magnificent animals walk in a natural setting.

The Northern Trail is another well-liked exhibit at the Woodland Park Zoo. Polar bears, reindeer, and arctic foxes are just a few of the creatures you can see in this exhibit that are indigenous to the Arctic and sub-Arctic. Visitors can get near these animals and see how they have evolved specifically to survive in frigid climates.

The Zoomazium in the Woodland Park Zoo is a must-see location for families with young children. The interactive exhibits and hands-on activities in this indoor play area teach children about animals and the natural world. It is intended for children under the age of eight. For added entertainment, the Zoomazium also has a storytelling area and a puppet theater.

Park Discovery

Discovery Park is a 534-acre nature reserve and recreational area in Seattle that is situated on the Puget Sound shoreline. This park offers miles of hiking routes, breathtaking vistas of the mountains and water, and several opportunities to see wildlife.

The West Point Lighthouse is one of Discovery Park's key draws. Built-in 1881, this antique lighthouse is still in function today. The lighthouse offers guided tours where visitors can learn about its background and local significance.

Bird viewing is another well-liked activity at Discovery Park. The park is a popular spot for bird aficionados as it is home to over 270 different species of birds. Hikers may explore the park's paths while keeping an eye out for ospreys, bald eagles, and other bird species.

The park also has a beach area where guests can stroll along the sand and look for marine life in the tidal pools. It's a wonderful chance for students to get knowledge of marine ecology and the species that live there.

The Flight Museum

The Museum of Flight is a top-notch aviation museum that's ideal for families with kids who love planes and space, and it's situated in the city of Tukwila, just south of Seattle.

The Space Gallery is one of the Museum of Flight's key draws. The Apollo 17 command module and a full-scale replica of the Space Shuttle are two examples of the artifacts and displays on display in this exhibition linked to space exploration. Visitors can discover more about the past, present, and future of space exploration.

The Great Gallery is another well-liked display at the Museum of Flight. More than 80 aircraft, including military aircraft, passenger jets, and experimental aircraft, are on display in this exhibition. Visitors have the opportunity to interact closely with these aircraft while learning about their history, design, and manufacture.

The Museum of Flight offers a variety of interactive activities and programs for youth interested in aviation and space, including summer camps with a space theme and flight simulators.

Families seeking an exciting and informative vacation should choose Seattle. There is something for everyone to enjoy in this area because of its abundance *of natural beauty, rich history, and vibrant cultural environment. There are several family-friendly* sites to check out, from the well-known Space Needle to the interactive displays at the Pacific Science Center and the Woodland Park Zoo. Seattle has much to offer whether you're interested in science, the outdoors, or aviation. So gather the family, pack your luggage, and get ready to see all that this incredible city has to offer!

Chapter 9: Seattle Outside

Seattle, Washington is renowned for its breathtaking natural beauty and abundance of outdoor recreation possibilities. In this busy and dynamic city, there is something for everyone to enjoy, including hiking, kayaking, skiing, riding, and beachcombing. We'll look at some of the top outdoor activities in Seattle and the surrounding areas in this article.

Seattle hiking

Seattle is surrounded by a stunning array of natural features, including the majestic mountains of the Cascade and Olympic ranges, lush forests, and clear lakes. Hiking is a well-liked activity among both locals and tourists due to the abundance of scenic beauty.

In the vicinity of Seattle, Mount Rainier National Park is one of the most well-liked places to go trekking. This park, which is home to Mount Rainier's recognizable peak, has a vast network of trails for hikers of all experience levels. Try the Skyline Trail for a strenuous day hike; it offers expansive views of the surrounding area and lots of opportunities for wildlife spotting. The Wonderland Trail, a 93-mile loop around Mount Rainier and provides unrivaled views of the peak and its glaciers, is another well-liked climb.

Consider hiking around Seattle's Discovery Park for a more urban experience. The largest park in the city, at 534 acres, has kilometers of pathways that go through wooded areas, open meadows, and breathtaking coastline cliffs. The Olympic Mountains, Mount Rainier, and Puget Sound can all be seen beautifully from the park.

Seattle kayaking

Due to the abundance of rivers and breathtaking natural landscape in the city, kayaking is another well-liked outdoor sport in *Seattle. In the center of Seattle, a freshwater lake* called Lake Union is one of the most well-liked places to go kayaking. Paddlers have access to Gas Works

Park, a former gas plant turned park with breathtaking views of Lake Union and the neighborhood, as well as views of the city skyline from this location.

The Puget Sound, a saltwater inlet with breathtaking views of the Olympic Mountains and the Seattle cityscape, is another well-liked kayaking location. Paddlers can explore the many coves, inlets, and islands that make up this lovely waterway by launching from several spots around the sound, such as Alki Beach, West Seattle, and Golden Gardens Park.

Observing whales in Seattle

Due to its proximity to the San Juan Islands and the Salish Sea, Seattle is among the top locations in the world for whale viewing. Whale-watching excursions leaving Seattle gives you the chance to get up and personal with these majestic creatures. The Salish Sea is home to several whale species, including orcas, humpbacks, and gray whales.

The San Juan Islands, a group of islands north of Seattle, is one of the most well-liked places to go whale watching. San Juan Safaris and Puget Sound Express are two tour companies that offer whale-watching excursions out of Seattle. They both provide a selection of trips and packages for whale-watching lovers.

Seattle Bicycling

Thanks to the city's large network of bike lanes and bike-friendly streets, biking is a well-liked form of transportation in Seattle. There are many possibilities to tour Seattle and its surroundings on two wheels, whether you're a casual cyclist or an avid mountain biker.

The Burke-Gilman track, a 27-mile track that runs from Seattle's Gas Works Park to the city of Bothell, is one of the most well-liked places to bike in Seattle. The trail offers breathtaking views of Lake Washington and the Cascade Mountains and follows the path of a historic railway line.

Mountain cyclists may find miles of trails and attractions at the Duthie Hill Mountain Bike Park in Issaquah, which is located just east of Seattle. The park offers beginner-friendly tracks as well as jumps, berms, and technical elements for more experienced riders.

Snowboarding and Skiing Near Seattle

While Seattle is renowned for its warm climate and frequent downpours, several ski resorts offer world-class skiing and snowboarding that are easily accessible from the city. About two hours southeast of Seattle, Crystal Mountain, is one of the most well-known resorts. Skiers and snowboarders of all abilities may find something to enjoy at Crystal Mountain, which has more than 2,600 acres of skiable terrain and receives 486 " of snow on average annually.

Stevens Pass is another well-known ski area close to Seattle and is situated about 90 minutes northeast of the city. Stevens Pass offers some of the best skiing and snowboarding in the Pacific Northwest with over 1,125 acres of skiable terrain and 460 inches of snowfall annually.

Beaches and waterfront parks in Seattle

Many beaches and waterfront parks can be found in Seattle, giving tourists the chance to relax in the sun and take in the breathtaking natural beauty of the city's coastline. Alki Beach, which is found in the West Seattle district, is one of the most well-known beaches. There are many options for sunbathing, swimming, and beach volleyball at this sandy beach, which also offers breathtaking views of the Olympic Mountains and the Seattle skyline.

Golden Gardens Park, which is situated in the Ballard area, is another well-liked waterfront park. This park includes picnic spots, a sandy beach, and breathtaking views of the Olympic Mountains and Puget Sound. The adjacent Golden Gardens Paddle Club offers kayak and paddleboard rentals for people who want to explore Puget Sound.

Natural splendor and outdoor adventure abound in Seattle. In this busy and dynamic city, there is something for everyone to enjoy, including hiking, kayaking, skiing, riding, and beachcombing. Get outside and enjoy everything this amazing city has to offer, whether you're a native looking to explore your neighborhood or a guest looking to experience the best of what Seattle has to offer.

Chapter 10: How to Navigate Seattle

Both locals and visitors can travel in a variety of ways throughout the city of Seattle. Seattle has a variety of options for getting around, including public transportation, bike share programs, taxis, shuttle buses, and vehicle rentals, in addition to walking and bicycling. We shall thoroughly examine Seattle's many modes of transportation in this article.

Seattle's public transportation system

Buses, light rail, and streetcars are all part of Seattle's public transit system. The buses are run by King County Metro Transit and travel all around the city and connect to other areas of the county. Sound Transit, the city of Seattle's light rail system, connects the downtown area with the airport and has plans to grow in the future. King County Metro also runs the streetcar, which travels from South Lake Union to Pioneer Square.

With more than 200 routes and more than 8,000 stops, the bus system in Seattle is enormous. Most bus lines operate from early in the morning until late at night, while *others run continuously. Bus fares are based on distance and the time of day, and there are discounts* for kids, pensioners, and individuals with disabilities. All public transit in the Seattle area accepts payments made with the ORCA card, a smart card.

The first line of Seattle's light rail system opened for service in 2009. There are now two lines: the Red Line connects Seattle to the University of Washington and the Blue Line travels from downtown Seattle to SeaTac Airport. In the upcoming years, Sound Transit intends to increase the light rail network. New lines are being planned for Northgate, Bellevue, and Redmond.

Programs for Bike Sharing in Seattle

Lime, JUMP, and Spin are just a few of the bike share programs available in Seattle. Through these schemes, users can borrow bicycles for a brief time and return them to predetermined places around the city. Since the bikes include GPS technology, consumers can easily locate and rent them using their smartphones.

Seattle's bike share services are reasonably priced, with rides costing between $1 and $2. For unlimited rides, users can also purchase monthly or yearly passes. These activities are a terrific way to see the city while also getting some exercise.

Seattle's Uber and Lyft

Users of the well-liked ride-sharing services Uber and Lyft in Seattle can quickly and easily request a trip using their cell phones. Standard rides, shared rides, and upscale rides are all available through both services. The cost of these services varies according to the demand, distance, and time of day.

At SeaTac Airport as well as other locations in the city, Uber and Lyft are accessible. These services are an excellent way to navigate the city without having to drive or search for parking. They are a practical choice for transportation in the early morning or late at night.

Shuttles and Taxis in Seattle

Another alternative for mobility in Seattle is the availability of taxis and shuttles. Taxis can be requested on the street or in advance with several different taxi companies. Taxi fares are governed by the city, with a $2.60 minimum fare and a $2.70 per mile rate.

Another transit choice in Seattle is the shuttle service, particularly for groups or individuals going to and from the airport. In the city, several shuttle services provide flat-rate, door-to-door service.

Renting a car in Seattle

Several rental vehicle businesses are active in Seattle, making it possible to rent a car there as well. If you want to explore the city and its surroundings at your own pace, renting a car is a terrific alternative. The company, the car type, and the length of the rental all affect the rental rates.

Pedaling a bike and walking in Seattle

In places with high traffic, biking, and walking are both excellent ways to explore Seattle. With a large number of bike lanes and paths all across the city, Seattle is renowned for being a bike-friendly city. The Burke-Gilman Trail, the Seattle Waterfront, and the Alki Trail are a few well-known bicycle paths.

The Pike Place Market and the Seattle Center are just two of the numerous pedestrian-friendly sites in Seattle. The best way to discover the city's areas and take in its distinctive culture is by walking.

Public transit, bike share programs, ride-sharing services, taxis, shuttles, automobile rentals, as well as walking and bicycling, are all available in Seattle. The ideal solution relies on the tastes and circumstances of the individual and has advantages and cons for each.

Conclusion

The booming metropolis of Seattle is situated in the American Pacific Northwest. The region is renowned for its breathtaking natural beauty, top-notch gastronomy, and diverse arts and music scene. There are several must-see sites in Seattle that you shouldn't *miss if you're thinking about taking a trip there. This* article will present a summary of Seattle's key attractions, some parting comments on visiting the city, some helpful links and information, a travel glossary, and a section with frequently asked questions.

Summary of Seattle's Top Attractions

The Space Needle is one of Seattle's most recognizable structures. Visitors can ride the elevator to the top of the Space Needle to take in the breathtaking views of the city and surroundings.

Pike Place Market: Pike Place Market is a thriving market that sells a variety of fresh produce, fish, and other things. Visitors can sip coffee at the original Starbucks or watch fishmongers hurl fish.

Chihuly Garden and Glass: This extraordinary museum showcases the magnificent glass creations of Dale Chihuly. A lovely outdoor garden with a variety of plants and water elements is also available at the museum.

The Museum of Pop Culture, usually referred to as MoPOP, is a unique museum that honors the background and tradition of popular music, science fiction, and pop culture.

Seattle Art Museum: The Seattle Art Museum is a well-known institution that houses a variety of international works of art. Everything from ancient antiquities to modern artwork is available for visitors to view.

Pioneer Square is Seattle's oldest district and is home to a variety of historic structures, art galleries, and one-of-a-kind stores and eateries.

Kerry Park: Kerry Park has some of the nicest views of the mountains and Seattle's skyline. Picnicking is permitted, or visitors can just take in the breathtaking scenery.

Boats can travel through the Hiram M. Chittenden Locks, sometimes referred to as the Ballard Locks, which are a remarkable feat of engineering that connects Lake Washington and Puget Sound.

The Seattle Great Wheel is a colossal Ferris wheel that provides breathtaking views of the city and its surroundings.

Seattle Aquarium: Anyone with a passion for aquatic life must visit the Seattle Aquarium. Diverse marine life, such as sharks, sea otters, and octopuses, are visible to visitors.

Last Words on Traveling to Seattle

Visitors will find Seattle to be a beautiful city with lots to do. Everyone can find something to enjoy in Seattle, regardless of their interests, whether they are in nature, culture, or just fantastic food and drink. Seattle can, however, get hectic and packed, *just like any other city, especially during the busiest travel times. To avoid disappointment on your* trip to Seattle, it's crucial to reserve your lodging and activities well in advance. To make moving around the city easier, it's a good idea to become familiar with the city's public transit system.

Information & Resources for Travel to Seattle

Travelers planning a vacation to Seattle have access to a wide range of services. Start by visiting Visit Seattle, the city's official tourism website. The website provides comprehensive information about sights, lodgings, and dining choices. The website has a blog as well, which offers advice and suggestions for travelers.

The Seattle Times, which provides a thorough guide to the city's attractions, eateries, and events, is another helpful source. The website includes a travel section with articles on the top accommodations, activities, and more.

The Washington Trails Association is a fantastic source of information for individuals interested in hiking and camping. For hikers and other outdoor lovers, the website provides a variety of trail descriptions, maps, and other helpful information.

Seattle Travel Terminology

When visiting Seattle, it's helpful to be aware of the following terms:

Puget Sound, a sizable body of water that encircles Seattle and the surrounding area, is referred to here as the "sound."

Seattle's moniker, Emerald City, derives from the city's luxuriant flora.

Based on the city's area code, Seattle is referred to as "The 206."

Seattle's reputation for having rainy weather has earned the city the moniker "Rain City."

Salmon: Salmon is a widely consumed cuisine in Seattle, which is renowned for its mouthwatering salmon dishes.

Coffee: The city of Seattle is well-known for its coffee, and it is also the location of several renowned coffee shops, including the first Starbucks.

Travel FAQ for Seattle

When is the ideal season to travel to Seattle?
The summer months, from June through August, are the finest for travel to Seattle. There are many outdoor things to enjoy and the weather is nice and sunny.

- *How can I travel around Seattle the most effectively?*

- *Seattle has an extensive public transit network that includes streetcars, light rail, and buses. Additionally, guests can rent a car or use ride-sharing services like Uber or Lyft.*

- *Which Seattle day outings are the most well-liked?*

- *Popular day trips from Seattle include exploring the adjacent islands, going to Bellevue or Tacoma, or going to nearby national parks like Mount Rainier or Olympic National Park.*

- *How is the climate in Seattle?*
- *The year-round pleasant and temperate weather in Seattle features cold temperatures and regular rainfall. Winters are chilly and rainy, but summers are pleasant and sunny.*

Seattle Tourism Board's contact details are as follows:

Visit Seattle is located at 701 Pike Street, Suite 800, Seattle, WA 98101, and can be reached at (206) 461-5840.

Visitors can find enough to enjoy in Seattle, which is a lively and dynamic city. Everyone can find something to enjoy in Seattle, regardless of their interests, whether they are in nature, culture, or just fantastic food and drink. To guarantee a seamless and enjoyable vacation, make sure to see some of the city's must-see attractions and plan your trip.

Printed in Great Britain
by Amazon

24591613R00059